A Time To Plant

52 Children's Sermons

Teresa L. Major

CSS Publishing Company, Inc., Lima, Ohio

A TIME TO PLANT

Copyright © 1998 by
CSS Publishing Company, Inc.
Lima, Ohio

All rights reserved. No part of this publication may be reproduced in any manner whatsoever without the prior permission of the publisher, except in the case of brief quotations embodied in critical articles and reviews. Inquiries should be addressed to: Permissions, CSS Publishing Company, Inc., P.O. Box 4503, Lima, Ohio 45802-4503.

Scripture quotations are from the *New Revised Standard Version of the Bible*, copyright © 1989 by the Division of Christian Education of the National Council of the Churches of Christ in the USA. Used by permission.

Library of Congress Cataloging-in-Publication Data

Major, Teresa L., 1959-
   A time to plant : 52 children's sermons / Teresa L. Major.
     p. cm.
   ISBN 0-7880-1163-4 (pbk.)
   1. Children's sermons. I. Title.
BV4315.M34 1998   97-28493
252'.53—dc21   CIP

This book is available in the following formats, listed by ISBN:
    0-7880-1163-4   Book
    0-7880-1164-2   IBM 3 1/2
    0-7880-1165-0   Mac
    0-7880-1166-9   Sermon Prep

PRINTED IN U.S.A.

To John,
who taught me the value of childhood.

For everything there is a season, and a time
for every matter under heaven:
a time to be born, and a time to die;
a time to plant, and a time to pluck up what is planted.

Ecclesiastes 3:1-2

Preface

A Time To Plant is both a creation and a collection. While I have written each of these sermons in my own style and to fit my situation, it would not be honest to claim that all the ideas are original with me. Many seeds for sermons or stories have come my way simply through everyday experience. Other ideas have been harvested by listening, reading, and observing others. A few of the stories included in these pages ("The Kite And The Sailboat" and "Too Close To The Edge") are stories I have heard and reworked with a different twist; I have no idea where they originated, but I am grateful to the original creator for the opportunity to spin off material that continues to benefit children.

I have been delivering children's sermons each week for over ten years. I firmly believe that every age group is important to the life of the church and that one of the ways we can keep children involved is by actively including them in Sunday morning services. When a solid message is presented with enthusiasm and clarity, it is readily grasped by both children and adults. When the children's sermon is used as a tool to enhance worship while offering nurture and instruction, it can easily become one of the highlights of the worship hour.

I hope these children's sermons offer help with planning worship and I pray that you reap as many joys as I have by sharing the faith with little ones in your congregation.

Teresa L. Major

Table of Contents

1. Tug-Of-War — 13
   Ephesians 4:1-3
2. Harmony — 14
   Colossians 3:14
3. A Missing Piece — 16
   1 Corinthians 12:14
4. Pieces And Parts — 17
   1 Corinthians 12:14-21
5. The Kite And The Sailboat — 19
   Romans 8:28
6. Behavior In Worship — 21
   1 Corinthians 14:40
7. Keep Growing! — 23
   1 Peter 2:2-3
8. The Right Thing To Do — 25
   Psalm 119:1-3
9. Learning To Behave — 27
   Psalm 119:4-8
10. Discrimination — 29
    Galatians 3:28
11. God Looks At The Heart — 31
    1 Samuel 16:7
12. Judge Not — 33
    Matthew 7:1-5
13. Something To Hang On To — 35
    2 Corinthians 12:9a
14. The Inside And The Outside — 37
    1 Corinthians 15:50
15. The Right Answer — 39
    Lamentations 3:24
16. Nothing Is Impossible With God — 40
    Luke 1:37

17. Where Do Our Words Come From?   42
    Matthew 12:34b
18. Spice It Up   44
    Matthew 5:13
19. Sharing The Warmth   46
    1 John 4:21
20. The Power Source   48
    Acts 1:8
21. God Never Forgets   50
    Psalm 103:17-18
22. God, The Recycler   52
    2 Corinthians 5:17
23. Hand Signals   54
    Matthew 11:28-30
24. Traffic Signals   56
    Colossians 4:2
25. Figuring The Answers   58
    Proverbs 3:5-6
26. False Advertising   60
    Matthew 23:27-28
27. Believing What God Says   62
    Genesis 6:22
28. A Light In The Darkness   64
    Matthew 5:14-16
29. What Hat Do You Wear?   66
    Proverbs 20:11
30. How Much Protection Do You Have?   68
    Psalm 119:9-11
31. Do It To Them, Do It To Me   70
    Matthew 25:40, 45
32. All Tangled Up   72
    James 4:7
33. Doing What You Were Meant To Do   74
    Jeremiah 29:11
34. A Fresh Start   76
    Romans 3:23-24
35. Being Ready   78
    Matthew 24:36-44

36. Big Sin, Little Sin   80
   Luke 6:37-42
37. Stain Remover   82
   1 John 1:9
38. Trouble   84
   Psalm 34:14
39. Too Close To The Edge   86
   Proverbs 4:14-15
40. Change   88
   Isaiah 43:19
41. Serendipity!   90
   Matthew 6:33
42. Expectations   92
   Romans 15:7

Special Day Sermons

43. Gifts For Mom   94
   Proverbs 31:28
44. Thanks, Dad   96
   Exodus 20:12
45. Remembering Something Important   98
   1 Corinthians 11:23-26
46. Rise Again!   100
   Matthew 28:5-6
47. The Messenger   102
   Luke 2:8-14
48. I'm Somebody!   104
   Luke 2:8-11
49. Giving What You've Got   106
   Luke 2:1-7
50. Don't Forget Jesus   108
   Luke 2:10-11
51. The Best Presents   110
   Matthew 1:21
52. A Birthday Party   111
   Luke 2:11

1. Tug-Of-War

Scripture: Ephesians 4:1-3

Concept: Those of us who love God, especially those of us in the church, should pull together as a team. We should not pull against each other and we should not try to pull anyone down.

Preparation: Rope. (If possible, have some children or youth help demonstrate your point.)

I need a few helpers this morning. *(Select several children and/or youth, and arrange them in equal teams on each end of the rope.)* Have you ever seen a tug-of-war competition? There are two teams, one on each side of the rope. There is a line in the dirt or sometimes even a mud hole between the two teams. Each team pulls and pulls, just as hard as it can, using all of its strength to pull the other team across the line or into the mud. One team wins by making the other team cross the line or fall in the mud.

People often act as if they are playing tug-of-war. One group pulls and fights against another group or tries to make themselves look better by pulling others down. They are mean to each other and sometimes they even do cruel things to hurt one another. When people play tug-of-war, all they care about is winning. They don't care about who falls in the mud or who gets hurt.

But in the church things should be different. We should all be on the same team, all of us pulling on the same side, never trying to pull anyone down or into the mud. *(Have all the children or youth move to the same side of the rope.)* Because God loves us, we do our best to love one another. We may not agree on everything, but we all agree that we love God and we want to do what makes him happy, and that includes pulling together!

This week I want you to find ways of pulling together with others to make things better instead of pulling or fighting against them. I will be praying for you. God bless you.

2. Harmony

Scripture: Colossians 3:14

Concept: Life is more pleasant and enjoyable when we work and play together without fighting.

Preparation: Enlist the help of the pianist/organist or go to the piano yourself and have the children gather around you there. (To make things even more interesting and to involve more people, you may wish to ask for the choir's help — have them sing the notes rather than playing them on the piano.)
If you do not have any music background and plan to present this lesson without any help, have someone show you how to locate "C," "D," "E," and "G" on the keyboard.

Music has a lot to teach us about how to get along with one another. We can play one musical note all by itself and it sounds pretty. *(Strike "C" and stop.)* But if we play that one note over and over, we will get tired of it. *(Strike "C" repetitively.)* That poor, lonely note needs some company. Suppose we add another note. *(Strike "C" and "E" together a few times and hold for a moment.)* Hey, that's kind of nice! That lonely note is not alone anymore and those two notes sound good together.

But what happens if the notes begin to fight? *(Strike "C" and "D" together several times.)* Ouch! That almost hurts my ears. I don't want those notes to fight for very long! I don't like that sound. I think I like this better. *(Play "C" and "E" together again.)* Those two notes get along so well, maybe they would like to make another friend. *(Play the chord, "C," "E," "G" several times and hold.)* What a wonderful sound! It's so warm and friendly, and it's nice to hear. It makes me feel good just listening to it. That pleasant sound reminds me of friends who work and play together without fighting.

It's all right to be by yourself sometimes *(strike "C")* and occasionally you may get into arguments with others *(strike "C" and "D" together)*, but you will be most happy when you spend your time working, playing, and sharing with your friends! *(Briskly strike "C," "E," "G" one note at a time and hold.)*

God bless you. Go make some beautiful music with your friends this week.

3. A Missing Piece

Scripture: 1 Corinthians 12:14

Concept: Like a puzzle that is missing a piece, the church is not whole when someone is missing.

Preparation: A children's puzzle with ten or fewer pieces (a puzzle of a church would be helpful — you can easily make one if necessary) and a flat surface on which to assemble the puzzle.

Do you like puzzles? I have a puzzle for us to work together this morning. I'm going to need your help. *(Distribute puzzle pieces and assist the children as needed. Be sure to withhold one piece of the puzzle.)* I can't wait to see our puzzle when it's finished!

We seem to have a problem. Our puzzle is not finished; it has a hole in it. It doesn't look right without all its pieces. Does someone have the missing piece? How can our puzzle be complete if we are missing a piece? This is disappointing!

Don't you hate it when a puzzle doesn't have all its pieces or a game is missing some parts? Things don't work right when all the parts are not there. It's just not the same. It is like that in the church, too. When you and your family are not here, we are like a puzzle that is missing a piece. You have an important place here; you are very special to us and when you are missing, we are not complete.

What is this in my pocket? *(Pull out the missing piece and put it in the appropriate place.)* There, that's much better. All the pieces are in place. I hope you like it here at Sunday School and church, and I hope to see you in your place every week because things just are not the same without you!

You will be in my prayers this week and I hope you will pray for me, too. God bless you.

4. Pieces And Parts

Scripture: 1 Corinthians 12:14-21

Concept: Just as all the parts are important to the body, so all the parts of the church (Christ's body) are important.

Preparation: A picture of a hand, foot, eye, and ear. Be familiar with 1 Corinthians 12:1-26.

(Display pictures one at a time, or if you have enough children, have four of them stand in front and hold the pictures.) Can you tell what these are? *(Children respond.)* Pictures of a hand, foot, eye, and ear. Look at these pictures for a moment, and tell me which one of them is most important to your body. What do you think, which one is most important? *(Allow answers one at a time.)* It is kind of difficult to decide which one is most important. If you didn't have a hand, it would be tough to play the piano or cut your food. If you didn't have a foot, you could still get around but it wouldn't be the same. Not being able to see would really change your life, and losing your hearing would close out a big part of your world.

Hmm, it seems like they are all important. There is a man in the Bible named Paul who tried to teach us some things about the body. Paul said that our bodies have many parts, and that all the parts belong to the same body. He was right. We have hands and feet, eyes and ears, noses and lips, and so on, and all those parts belong to our body. The whole body is not made up of just one part, is it? We'd look pretty silly if we were just one big nose or one big foot. We need all the parts to be a complete body.

Paul said the church was like the body of Christ, and it needed all its parts to be a whole body. Our bodies need all their parts to work correctly and the church needs all its parts to work smoothly. What if the church only had preachers? What if the church only had people who could work in the nursery or who could only serve in the kitchen? What if the church only had people who could meet others at the door or who could sing in the choir? Do you see the problem? We need *all* the parts.

Paul knew what he was talking about. Our bodies have lots of parts and each one is important, but none of them is more important than the others. It takes all the parts for the body to work best. It's the same with the church. The church, the body of Christ, is made up of many parts, and each part has a special job to do. The church cannot work as it's supposed to if some of the parts are missing.

Make sure you are at church to do your part, because you are important, and the church, the body of Christ, is not the same when you are not here! God bless you.

5. The Kite And The Sailboat

Scripture: Romans 8:28

Concept: If we try hard enough, we can find something good, even in bad situations.

Preparation: None.

Has anything bad ever happened to you? Bad things happen to all of us; there is nothing we can do about that. But there is something we can do about our attitudes when bad things happen. Let me tell you a story.

Jerry spent all day working on his sailboat. He had built it piece by piece, all by himself. It had taken him a long time to paint it and to carefully put on the sails. He was so proud of his work. But now the paint was dry and the sailboat was finished and Jerry could hardly wait to go to the park and sail his boat in the lake.

Jerry arrived at the park and searched for the best place to launch his masterpiece. He walked down to the edge of the lake and gently set his sailboat on the water. What a beautiful sight! His boat began to move gracefully through the ripples. But oh, no! A blustering wind began to blow and before Jerry could rescue his boat, the wind had crashed it into some rocks. The little sailboat was broken into a thousand pieces. All of Jerry's hard work was ruined.

Jerry bent down and picked up the pieces of his broken sailboat and said, "You know, it's not a very good day to sail sailboats, but it looks like a terrific day to fly a kite!" And with that, he ran home to get his kite and returned to have a wonderful afternoon watching the kite dance in the clouds.

Jerry could have gotten angry and thrown a temper tantrum. He could have sat down by the lake and cried, but instead Jerry found something good in a bad situation.

You see, it's all in how we look at things. We can find something good in almost any situation if we'll just try.

God bless you. Remember to pray for one another this week.

6. Behavior In Worship

Scripture: 1 Corinthians 14:40

Concept: When we misbehave in worship, not only do we miss out, but we keep others from participating in the service.

Preparation: None.

Have you ever tried to watch your favorite television show or play your favorite video game while people were interrupting you? Maybe they kept getting in front of the screen, or they made a lot of noise, or they just kept asking you questions so you could not concentrate. Doesn't it irritate you when that happens?

This morning I want to talk to you about something far more important than watching television or playing a video game. I want to talk to you about our behavior during the worship service. Why do you think people come here every Sunday? *(Allow children to explain their answers.)* People come here to worship God. They come to show God how much they love him by praying, singing, giving, and by listening to God's word when the sermon is preached. People come to share with others who love God. What we do here on Sunday morning is very important.

Sometimes people come to worship and something keeps them from doing so. Do you have any idea what might keep someone from being able to worship? It's noise, and many times that noise is coming from boys and girls who are not behaving. You see, when you crawl under the pews, or make a lot of noise, or talk to your mom and dad, or keep going in and out, or wiggle around, you disturb those around you. Some people cannot pray when there is noise or commotion. Some people can't concentrate on the sermon and some just can't worship God if things are loud.

It really is not fair for any of us to keep someone else from being able to worship. What do you think we can do to make sure our church is a place where people really can worship God? *(Help children with appropriate responses.)* We can sit quietly and pay attention to what's going on. We can stay in our seat and not crawl under the pews or walk around the aisles. We can go to the restroom before the service starts so we will not have to leave. We can keep our hands to ourselves and not fight with our brothers and sisters.

It is important that everyone have a chance to hear about God and God's love and that everyone be able to worship. I know I can count on you to behave in the service so that our church is a special place to worship and praise the Lord.

Have a good week. Invite someone to come with you to Sunday School and church next week. God bless you.

7. Keep Growing!

Scripture: 1 Peter 2:2-3

Concept: Growth is important in all areas of life.

Preparation: None.

Do any of you have baby brothers or sisters at home? Have all of you seen a little baby? They're so cute and cuddly, but they need lots of help; they can't do anything for themselves.

Have you ever watched babies learn to eat? What a mess! They get food all over the floor, all over their clothes, and all over themselves. It's in their hair, it's in their ears, it's everywhere! But eventually, they get a little better and don't spill so much on the floor and before you know it, they're able to handle a spoon like the big kids.

How about when they are trying to learn to walk? Don't they look adorable wobbling all around the floor? They take a few steps, then boom, down they go! But they practice and practice, taking just a few steps each time, and soon they're able to run all over the house.

Babies are cute when they're little and just learning how to eat and walk. But if a baby stays like a baby and never learns how to eat or walk by himself, there is a big problem. Something is wrong if a baby doesn't begin to grow and learn.

Babies grow bit by bit. We can see the changes in *them* as they grow, but it is important for *us* to grow as well. We not only grow by getting taller and bigger, we grow by what we learn and how we behave. When we are little, we understand God as a child and we behave like a child and that is good. But as we grow up, we should see our understanding of God grow. Our behavior should change to show that we are growing and learning.

If you've been coming to Sunday School and church for a long time, you know more now about how God wants you to live than you did when you were a young child. Am I right? That's good. That's how it's supposed to be. As you grow, your relationship with God should be growing, too.

This week, I'm going to pray that you will continue to grow up strong and healthy and that your relationship with the Lord will continue to grow as well. God bless you.

8. The Right Thing To Do

Scripture: Psalm 119:1-3

Concept: We need to do what is right simply because it's the right thing do, not just to stay out of trouble.

Preparation: None.

There are many ways to tell if you're growing up. One way is to measure how tall you've gotten. Another more important way is to see what kind of decisions and choices you are making and how you are behaving.

Let me ask you a question. What is a rule? *(Children respond. Offer help and clarification as needed.)* A rule is something that helps us know what we are supposed to do. Is that right? Why do we have rules? *(Children respond.)* Ah, we have rules to make us behave a certain way. One more question, why should we obey the rules? *(Children respond. Undoubtedly, you will hear, "We obey the rules so we won't get in trouble." Listen carefully to hear, "We obey the rules because it is the right thing to do." If the children do not come up with this answer, be sure to supply it.)*

There seem to be two main reasons that we obey rules. The first reason is we don't want to get in trouble. That makes sense. Who wants to get in trouble for doing something wrong? Who wants to be punished?

The second reason is because we know obeying the rules is the right thing to do. Let's think about this one for a moment. If you could do something wrong and you knew you would not get caught, would you do it? Some of us might. Some of us might try to see what we could get away with, especially if we knew we would not get in trouble. But is that the right thing to do? Should we break the rules just because we know we will not get caught? No.

Those of us who are growing up and trying to make decisions that will make God happy will choose to do the right thing, even if we can get away with doing the wrong thing. Growing up the way God wants us to means living the way God wants instead of living the way we want. It means making decisions and choices that help us obey God's rules for our lives.

It's good to obey the rules so we will not get in trouble, but it is even better to obey the rules simply because we know it's the right thing to do.

This week, I challenge you to follow the rules, because you know that's what God would want you to do. God bless you.

9. Learning To Behave

Scripture: Psalm 119:4-8

Concept: We can spray hair spray on our hair to make it behave and do what it's supposed to do, but we have to make ourselves behave by making good decisions and doing what is right.

Preparation: A container of hair spray.

Does anyone know what this is? *(Hold up hair spray. Children respond.)* It's hair spray. What do you do with hair spray? *(Children respond.)* You spray it all over your hair and the hair spray makes it stay in place. The hair spray makes your hair behave.

Some days I get up and get dressed and fix my hair, but it won't do what it's supposed to do. I fuss with it, and comb it and brush it. I use the curling iron on it, but it wants to be stubborn and cantankerous. This piece sticks up here *(demonstrate)* and this piece is flopping around over here, and this part won't do anything. But, I can spray a little hair spray on it and *force* it to behave. I can *make* it do what I want it to do.

If you spray hair spray all over yourself, will it make you behave? That's ridiculous, isn't it? Of course hair spray can't make us behave. It might help our hair, but it will not help our behavior. If hair spray can't help, who or what makes us behave? *(Children respond.)* I heard several answers. Somebody said God makes us behave. Someone said our moms, dads, and teachers make us behave. Someone else said we make ourselves behave.

Let's talk about your answers. Does God make us behave? Not really. God lets us choose what we are going to do, even when we choose the wrong thing. God wants us to behave, but God leaves that decision up to us.

Do our moms, dads, and teachers make us behave? No. They teach us right from wrong and they help us learn what is expected of us. They correct us when we mess up and they may even punish us to help us learn, but when you get right down to it, they can't really *make* us behave. They can teach us, correct us, and even punish us, but who is really responsible for whether we behave or not? *(Point to self.)* We are. Each of us has to make the choice about how we are going to behave.

When we misbehave and don't do what we are supposed to do, not only do we get in trouble, but we also hurt God. He wants us to do what is right so that our lives can be happy and full.

There is no hair spray that can make us behave. We have to take the time to think about what we are doing, so we can make good choices and decisions about our behavior.

I'll pray for you and you pray for me this week. God bless you.

10. Discrimination

Scripture: Galatians 3:28

Concept: God made everyone and we hurt God when we judge others unfairly because of things they can't help.

Preparation: A bag of candy or stickers. (Something that can be used as a small gift. Make sure you have enough for everyone.) *You'll have to think on your feet for this one. The attributes or characteristics you use in this lesson will have to be chosen quickly, depending on the children present.*

Hmm, let me look you over this morning. Here, you *don't* have blonde hair, you can have a present. *(Give children who do not have blonde hair candy or stickers.)* I don't like blonde hair. I heard that all people with blonde hair are mean. People with blonde hair can't have a present. Oh, here, you *don't* have blonde hair, you get a present. *(Go to the children one by one making observations about them.)*

Well, that's enough blonde hair. How about white socks? Who has on white socks? Too bad. You have on white socks. You don't get a gift. *(Pass over all the children wearing white socks, giving gifts to all the other children.)* I heard that everyone who wears white socks is bad. Sorry. You have on white socks. You can't have a gift.

Some of you don't look too happy about all of this. What's the matter? How did it feel to be skipped over or left out just because you have blonde hair or because you wore white socks this morning? *(Allow children to share their feelings.)*

So you don't think it's fair that some people got a special gift and others didn't just because they looked different? You know what? You are exactly right. It is not fair for people to be left out or treated unfairly just because of how they look. But you know what else? Many people treat others that way all the time.

People get judged unfairly because their skin is a different color or because they weigh more than other people. Some people get judged unfairly because they don't have a lot of money and they dress differently than others, or because they are girls instead of boys. Do you see how wrong it is to judge people based on how they look on the outside? Can you understand how much it can hurt someone to be treated so unfairly?

If we believe in God and we love God, then we also believe that God created each and every one of us. If God made all of us, then no one has the right to treat anyone else unfairly because of looks.

You have been good sports this morning. If you did not get a present earlier, you may have one now because you are all special to God and to me, no matter what you look like.

This week, be very careful not to treat anyone unfairly just because they look different. God bless you.

11. God Looks At The Heart

Scripture: 1 Samuel 16:7

Concept: When God looks at a person, God is more concerned with what's on the inside than with what's on the outside.

Preparation: Be familiar with 1 Samuel 16:1-12. If possible, have three or four older boys or youth help with this lesson.

The Bible tells us a story about a time when Israel needed a new king. God sent a man named Samuel to find the new ruler. Samuel was a good man who had helped God in many ways, and God told Samuel that he would point him in the right direction and would let him know when he had found the right person to be king.

God told Samuel to go and find a man named Jesse. Jesse had many sons and one of them was God's choice to be the new king. Jesse called his sons in one by one to meet Samuel. *(If you have older boys or youth helping, have them come up one by one as you finish the story.)* First came a strong, young man, but the Lord said to Samuel, "No, this is not the one." Next came another good-looking, strapping young fellow, but he was not God's choice either. A third son came in to see Samuel but Samuel said, "No, this one has not been chosen," The Bible says that Jesse had seven of his sons pass before Samuel but none of them was God's choice.

Samuel finally asked Jesse if all of his sons had come in to see him. Jesse said, "Yes, these are all my sons except my youngest boy, David, who is out caring for the sheep."

Samuel asked Jesse to send for David, the young, small boy who was out in the field. When David came to see Samuel, God let Samuel know that he was the one.

David would be the new king. This was a surprise to Jesse and his older, stronger, and wiser sons. It was even a surprise to Samuel. Jesse had many older sons who looked like they would make better kings, but the Lord said to Samuel, "Don't be so concerned with how someone looks. Don't worry so much about how tall or how big someone is. People look at the outside, but God looks at the heart."

God did not care how big or how small David was. God was concerned with what was in David's heart and God knew that David was a good young man. He was God's choice to be the new king.

Sometimes we feel that we don't matter because we are young or small, but God doesn't care what we look like on the outside. God cares about what kind of person we are on the inside, and if God has a special job for us to do, he will help us do it, no matter what. Remember, people look at the outside, but God looks at the inside. God looks at our heart.

God bless you. Have a great week.

12. Judge Not

Scripture: Matthew 7:1-5

Concept: Sometimes we have a difficult time seeing what we do wrong because we are too busy judging others' wrongdoings.

Preparation: A pen or marker. Prepare the following list, printed at the top of a sheet of paper: Took two cookies, did not brush teeth, laughed at my doll, made fun of my dress, did not clean room. Be familiar with Matthew 7:1-5.

    I would like to tell you a story this morning about a brother and a sister, Mary and Jack. Mary ran to Mother one Saturday morning, shouting, "Mother, Mother, come look at my list! Here are all the reasons you should punish Jack today. He has been bad. I watched him and I wrote down everything he did wrong. Mother, you should make him stay in his room and take away his bike and not let him talk on the phone!"
    "My goodness," said Mother. "Let me have a look at your list." *(Hold up paper and read the list aloud.)* "Took two cookies, did not brush teeth, laughed at my doll, made fun of my dress, did not clean room. Seems like your brother may have to face some consequences because of what he has done, but before I punish him, I need to print your list, Mary."
    Mother took out a pen and drew a line across the paper under Mary's writing. *(Hold up the paper and draw a line to separate Jack's list and Mary's list.)* "My list! What are you talking about, Mother, what list?" Mary protested. "Let's see," Mother said as she began writing. "Did not feed the cat, said ugly things to Jack, was mean to a neighbor, was a tattletale, did not make bed."
    "You have shown me what your brother has done wrong today, Mary," said Mother, "but you realize that if I punish Jack, I have to punish you, too."

Mother explained to Mary that she had spent so much time worrying about what her brother had done wrong that she had forgotten about all the wrong things she had done. Mother told Mary that she would punish Jack if Mary wanted to be punished as well. Mary decided to take the list, ball it up, and toss it into the trash can.

We act like Mary sometimes, don't we? We spend so much time watching others' mistakes that we forget about our own. The Bible tells us not to judge other people, because the way we judge them is the way we will be judged. The Bible says we also need to take a good look at ourselves and what we do wrong before we ever try to point out what someone else is doing wrong.

I don't know about you, but I mess up enough in my own life that I don't have any right to judge anyone else. This week, instead of looking at other people's mistakes, try to pay attention to your own. God bless you.

13. Something To Hang On To

Scripture: 2 Corinthians 12:9a

Concept: When we start to fall, Jesus is there for us to hang on to.

Preparation: A pair of ski poles, if possible. If not, help the children understand what ski poles are and what they are used for.

Have you ever seen any of these? *(Display poles.)* Do you know what they are used for? *(Children respond.)* These are ski poles and people use them when they go skiing down the mountain. They go swoosh! swoosh! and use these poles to help them keep their balance and to point them in the direction they want to go. *(Demonstrate by pretending you are skiing.)* If they want to turn a little, then they can use the poles to help them do that. If they begin to fall, they can use these poles to help them keep their balance so they won't take a tumble. And, if they do fall down, the skiers can even use these poles to help them get up.

That's a neat thing to have, isn't it? Something that helps us go where we want to go and helps us not fall down, and even helps us get up when we do fall. Wouldn't it be great if we had something or someone like that all the time — not just on the ski slopes? In a way, we do have someone like that.

When we have Jesus in our lives, and if we follow him, he helps us make good choices and decisions so we can go in the right direction. When things get hard and we feel like we are all alone or like we're falling down, Jesus can help us. During those bad times when we do fall and everything is going wrong, Jesus can help us get back on our feet. Jesus is someone we can hold on to all the time. He loves us and he wants to be there to help us, if we will let him.

Ski poles give us something to hold on to when we are skiing down a mountain, but Jesus is someone we can hold on to and someone we can trust to help us all the time.

Think about Jesus this week and let him help you. God bless you.

14. The Inside And The Outside

Scripture: 1 Corinthians 15:50

Concept: We spend a lot of time taking care of the outside of our bodies but sometimes we forget to take care of the inside.

Preparation: A shaving or cosmetic bag with deodorant, perfume or cologne, shampoo, soap, razor, comb, etc. Use as many items as desired.

Let's see what we've got in here. A bar of soap, what do we do with this? *(Children respond.)* Have you ever seen a man shave? We have a razor because we wouldn't want the men to have scruffy faces. How about this shampoo, what is this for? *(Children respond.)* Look at this, we have some deodorant because we would not want to smell bad. Ah, and a bottle of perfume (or cologne) because we want to smell good.

It is important to take care of our bodies. Its important to keep ourselves clean. We want to be sure we don't smell bad because no one would want to be around us. Ladies put on make-up and men shave their faces. We all take baths, brush our teeth, and comb our hair. We need to do these things.

But look at all this stuff we use to take care of the outside of our bodies. Soap, shampoo, combs, razors, perfume, make-up, all kinds of things. We spend a lot of time making sure the outside is neat and clean and that we look attractive and smell good. But many times we forget about the inside; we forget about our hearts.

If we are going to be the kind of people that God wants us to be, we have to spend at least as much time taking care of the inside as we do taking care of the outside. I'm not talking about eating right and exercising; those are very important, too, but I'm talking about taking care of our relationship with God.

There are several ways we can take care of our relationship with God. We can read our Bibles or have someone read Bible stories to us. We can come to Sunday School and church so we can learn more about Jesus. We can pray and talk with God about what's going on in our lives. We can treat other people the way we believe Jesus would want us to treat them.

It takes a lot of time to do all these things, but just as it is important to care for the outside of our bodies, it's even more important to care for the inside. Our relationship with the Lord is more important than anything else we do.

This week, make sure you spend time taking care of the outside, but spend even more time taking care of the inside. God bless you.

15. The Right Answer

Scripture: Lamentations 3:24

Concept: Jesus is the answer to life's problems.

Preparation: Several sheets of paper with the following math problems printed on them: 5+5=, 12-2=, 3+7=, 15-5=, 2+8=.

You are going to have to think this morning in order to help me with our lesson. Let's see how we do with these problems. Can you give me the answers? *(Hold up the problems, one at a time, and offer any help that may be needed.)*

Did you notice anything about these problems? *(Children respond.)* Even though we had a lot of problems to solve, they all had the same answer. The problems were all different, but the answer was always the same.

Did you know that life works that way for people who love and follow Jesus? Life has many problems, but if we trust Jesus and if we turn to him, we find that he is the answer to all of our problems and troubles. No matter how big or how small our problem is, Jesus can help.

If you feel lonely, Jesus can help you know that you are never alone. If you are afraid, Jesus can help you feel safe. If you get sick, Jesus can help you get better. If something really bad happens to you, and you feel feel hurt and sad, Jesus can help you get through the pain.

Jesus does not always take our problems away, even when we want him to, but he is the answer. No matter what kind of trouble we have, Jesus can make a difference in our lives if we will trust him, turn to him, and ask him to help us.

This week, I'm going to pray that you will remember to turn to Jesus when you have a problem to solve. God bless you.

16. Nothing Is Impossible With God

Scripture: Luke 1:37

Concept: Nothing is impossible with God's help.

Preparation: Be familiar with Luke 1:26-38. This lesson could of course be used as a pre-Christmas sermon, but it could be presented anytime.

I know it's not Christmastime, but this morning we are going to talk about the very beginning of the Christmas story. Does anyone remember what happened first? *(Children respond. Offer help as needed.)* The angel came and delivered some news to Mary. What did the angel tell Mary? *(Children respond.)* The angel told Mary not to be afraid because she had been chosen by God to do something special. The angel said that Mary was going to have a baby. This would be no ordinary baby; this baby would be God's son. The angel told Mary that this child would be different from other babies because God had some very important things for him to do.

What news this was from the angel! It was a miracle! But Mary must have been a bit confused and maybe even a little scared. It must have been difficult to understand everything the angel had said. How could it be? How could something like this happen to her? How could she be the mother of God's son?

The Bible tells us that the angel told Mary something else before he left. The angel said, "With God, nothing is impossible."

With God, nothing is impossible. Say that with me, "With God, nothing is impossible." Say it again, "With God, nothing is impossible." Do you believe that? It's true. No matter how impossible something seems, no matter how much we believe we cannot do something, if it's God's will, and if we are willing to try, nothing is impossible for us.

Imagine there is someone who is always mean to you. Maybe she says bad things to you or always tries to get you in trouble. You just can't stand this person, but you know God wants you to be nice to her. It seems impossible, doesn't it? But it's not. With God's help, you can do it.

Suppose God wants you to be a missionary when you grow up. Suppose he wants you to go far away and tell others about him and his love. Impossible? No. Why? Because, say it with me, "With God, nothing is impossible."

Mary was confused and afraid and she did not fully understand how something so important could be happening to her. It seemed impossible, but it did happen because — say it with me one more time, "With God, nothing is impossible!"

I want you to remember that. God bless you.

17. Where Do Our Words Come From?

Scripture: Matthew 12:34b

Concept: The words we speak come from who we are on the inside.

Preparation: Be familiar with Matthew 12:34.

Where do words come from? When you say something, where do you get the words? *(Children respond. Repeat their answers, encourage further responses, and add to their list if necessary.)* Someone said words come from our mouths, and our tongues. Somebody said words come from dictionaries, typewriters, and computers. I heard someone say words come from books. I also heard that words come from our brain. Those are all good answers, but there is one other place words come from that I want us to think about this morning. Did you ever stop to think that words come from our hearts?

Sounds kind of strange, doesn't it, words coming from our hearts? Hearts don't have lips. Hearts can't talk; they don't speak to us. But in many ways, our hearts are responsible for everything we say.

The Bible teaches us that the things we say come from what's in our hearts. The words we use and the things we say tell others a lot about us. If we are full of bitter, hateful talk, then our hearts are probably full of bitterness and hatred. If we use harsh, mean, and ugly words all the time, that's most likely what's in our hearts. If we speak kind and gentle words, our hearts are likely full of kindness and gentleness, and if we use words that show love and caring, we probably have hearts that are filled with love and care for other people.

What kind of talk comes out of your mouth and what does it say about you? Remember, the Bible teaches that the words that come out of our mouths actually tell others what is in our hearts.

Listen to yourself this week. Listen to what you are saying. Make sure your words come from a clean, pure heart. God bless you.

18. Spice It Up

Scripture: Matthew 5:13

Concept: As salt makes a difference in food, we, as Christian people, are called to make a difference in the world.

Preparation: A salt shaker.

What kinds of foods do you like to put salt on? *(Children respond. Acknowledge each response.)* We really like to put salt on scrambled eggs and french fries and popcorn. Anything else? French fries without salt taste kind of different, don't they? They taste kind of plain, like something is missing. The same with popcorn. It needs something to spice it up a little. And scrambled eggs, they're just no good without a little salt.

Salt spices things up. It adds flavor and taste to foods. It makes a difference to our taste buds. Certain foods just aren't the same without salt. Popcorn without salt; yuck, how boring.

The Bible tells us that we are the salt of the earth. That means that those of us who love God are here to make a difference in our world. We are here to add spice to life so that things don't seem so plain or boring. God wants us to spice things up, just by being around other people.

Salt is strong. It only takes a little to make a big difference. God wants us to make a difference by sharing our strength.

How can we be like salt? We can tell others about Jesus and how much he loves us. We can do nice things for people and we can help those who need us. We can be like salt by standing up for what is right even when everyone else chooses to do wrong. We can share how happy we are that we have Jesus in our lives. We can be like salt in the world by living lives that please God.

French fries, eggs, and popcorn just aren't the same without salt, and the world just wouldn't be the same without Christian people to spice it up! Go out and spice up your world this week. God bless you.

19. Sharing The Warmth

Scripture: 1 John 4:21

Concept: Like a radiator emanating warmth, the warmth, love, and joy of Christ should emanate from us.

Preparation: A picture of a radiator, if possible.

When you have been out in the snow building a snowman and you come inside with wet mittens and a red nose and frozen toes, what is the first thing you want to do? *(Children respond.)* Get warm! Of course. You want to get rid of that cold feeling and warm up. Sometimes, when I come in after being out in the cold, I like to stand in front of the radiator and warm my hands and feet. The heat rolls over me and before I know it, the cold has been chased away.

Have any of you ever seen a radiator? I have radiators in my house. They are special kinds of heaters connected to the wall with water running through them. The water inside gets hot and heats up the outside of the radiator. The hot radiator spreads its warmth over the whole room so things feel toasty and comfortable.

Christian people are like radiators. Inside we are filled with a special warmth and a special love because of Jesus. Because we love the Lord, we can't help but let some of the love and warmth come out. When we meet people who don't know about Jesus and how much he loves them, we should be like a radiator spreading the warmth.

There are so many people around us who are lonely and hurting and cold, and we could make a big difference in their lives if we would share the warmth we have inside. If we let our warmth and our love come through, we can chase away the cold and the chill that others feel.

Radiators heat up and spread the warmth around the room so everyone can enjoy it. We can be like radiators if we will let the warmth and the love of Jesus come through us so that others can feel it.

Be like a radiator this week, sharing the warmth inside you with others who need it. God bless you.

20. The Power Source

Scripture: Acts 1:8

Concept: A battery supplies the power and energy to many things, in much the same way that the Holy Spirit supplies power and energy to Christians.

Preparation: Any size battery.

(Display battery.) Do you know what this is? It's a battery. What do batteries do? *(Children respond.)* Batteries "run" things. They give power and energy to many items we use every day. My watch has a battery in it and so does my camera. What sorts of things do you have that use batteries? *(Video game, remote control, cassette player, cars, trucks, radios, dolls, etc.)* Wow, we use batteries in a lot of places, don't we? They give our belongings the power they need to work.

What happens when the batteries run down? *(Children respond.)* If the batteries run down our toy or game just stops. It will not work anymore because it does not have any power. It just sits there, doing nothing. My watch and my camera are not much good if they don't have any power. We can fix our things and give them new power by putting in new batteries. Wouldn't it be great if we had batteries that would never wear out?

Did you know that the Holy Spirit is like a battery for us? The Holy Spirit is a special part of God that helps us. He is like a battery that never wears out. He gives us power, energy, and strength. He keeps us going. When we think we can't do something, the Holy Spirit helps us get it done. When we have to deal with sad things that happen in our lives, he is there to give us strength. When people make fun of us and treat us badly, he gives us the power to deal with them.

When we are too tired to keep going, the Holy Spirit is our energy. When something terrific happens to us, he is there to celebrate with us. He gives us the ability to tell other people about Jesus. No matter what we need, he is there for us.

Through the Holy Spirit working in our lives we receive the power and strength we need to make it through every day. He is like a battery that never wears out and he never gets tired of helping us.

Ask God to give you the power or strength you need this week. God bless you.

21. God Never Forgets

Scripture: Psalm 103:17-18

Concept: We use many methods to help us remember lots of things, but God never forgets.

Preparation: A "To Do" list, a piece of string tied around your finger, and an activity calendar.

What do you do to help you remember things? *(Children respond.)* I hate to forget appointments or commitments, but sometimes I have so many things to do and so many places to be, I cannot keep everything straight in my head. I have to do something to help me remember.

Grown-ups have special ways of reminding themselves of what we need to remember. Some people tie a little piece of string around their finger. *(Hold up your finger with the string.)* When they notice the string, they are reminded of what they are supposed to do. Other people make themselves a "To Do" list everyday. *(Display a list written with large letters that can be read at a distance.)* This list says, "Go to the grocery store, doctor's appointment at 10:00 a.m., pick up package from post office, lunch date at 12:30," and so forth. This is my activity calendar. *(Display the calendar.)* It is like the "To Do" list except it shows all the days together. Do you see how all these things work? They remind us of what we are supposed to do and where we are supposed to be.

We hate to forget, but let me ask you a question. Has anyone ever forgotten to do something for you? It is disappointing when that happens. Maybe someone forgot to pick you up on time from a friend's house, or maybe they forgot to take you to the movies like they said they would. Whatever it was, it hurt to be forgotten.

There is someone who never forgets. There is someone who doesn't need a "To Do" list, or a piece of string tied on a finger, or an activity calendar, or anything else to help him remember us. Do you know who that is? *(Children respond.)* God. (Or Jesus.) God knows all about us. He knows everything we do, everything we think, and he goes everywhere we go. And, he never forgets to be with us. He never forgets what we need. He never forgets to love us. He never forgets to care. We can always count on him to remember us.

We might forget things, but God never forgets. He always remembers you. I'll be praying for you this week. Let me encourage you to pray for each other. God bless you.

22. God, The Recycler

Scripture: 2 Corinthians 5:17

Concept: Even when we make "garbage" of our lives, God can make that "garbage" into something beautiful and special.

Preparation: A large garbage bag with trash in it. (Empty soft drink cans, empty pizza boxes, old newspaper, etc.)

I have brought some trash to share with you this morning. What's the matter? You don't want to share my trash? Don't worry, it's clean. Here, you hold this can. *(Begin distributing some of the items.)* You hold this pizza box, and could you help me with this newspaper? All of these things are trash, but we can do something with this trash to make it usable again. Who knows what we can do? *(Children respond. Offer assistance if necessary.)* We can recycle much of our trash so it can be remade into something valuable. We have learned that we throw away too much stuff. We are wasteful. Now we know that if we put forth a little effort, we can recycle things over and over.

What kinds of things can be recycled? *(Children respond.)* Soft drink cans, paper, car tires, plastic jugs, glass, so many things can be recycled. These things can be made new again. What about people? Can people be recycled? That sounds like a strange question, doesn't it, but did you know that, in a way, people can be recycled?

We do all sorts of things that make trash out of our lives. We tell lies and cheat and we hurt ourselves by not taking care of our bodies. We hurt other people and we hurt God. We ignore the things that God has tried to teach us. We live the way we want instead of the way God wants, and soon our lives have been wasted. They are like trash, good for nothing. But God can take the trash and make a treasure.

Just as we recycle paper, tin cans, and plastic into something new and usable, God can take a broken and trashy life and recycle it into something beautiful and valuable. It does not matter what we have done wrong. God can make us new if we will tell him we are sorry for the wrong things we have done, and if we show him we are ready to live his way. He can remake our lives into something very special.

God wants us to be happy. He does not want our lives to be a trashy mess. God is the only one who can make us new.

As you recycle your trash this week, remember that God can recycle you! God bless you.

23. Hand Signals

Scripture: Matthew 11:28-30

Concept: We can use our hands to show what we are feeling.

Preparation: None.

Let's see if you can read my hand signals this morning. What does this mean? *(Wave. Children respond.)* I'm saying, "Hi!" How about this? *(Both hands in front of you, fingers pointing up, palms facing children. Children respond.)* This means, "Stop!" or "Back off, don't come any closer!" Let's try another one. *(Fold your hands and arms in front of you and drop your head. Children respond.)* This one could mean a lot of things, couldn't it? This might mean, "Leave me alone," or "I'm sad," or "I'm shy." Okay, two more. This is an easy one. *(Hands held in fists in a fighting stance. Children respond.)* No doubt about this one. It means, "Come on, I'm ready to fight!" Last one. *(Hands open as if beckoning someone to come to you. Children respond.)* This is a nice one. It means, "You can come to me. I care and I want to help you."

We can use our hands to say a lot of things. We can let people know we want to fight or that we care and want to give them a hug. Would you rather see this, or this? *(Fists or hug. Children respond.)* Me, too. Hugs are always better than fists.

The Bible tells us about a time when Jesus invited people to come to him. Jesus said, "Come to me, all of you who are tired and need comfort, and I will give you rest." Jesus invited the people to come to him to be helped, to rest, and to find someone who cared. I can almost picture Jesus in my mind, standing there with his hands and arms stretched out to the people. *(Demonstrate.)*

Jesus cares about us and he is there reaching out to us when we are tired, hurt, sad, or lonely. He will never do this to us when we come to him. *(Demonstrate "Stop, don't come any closer" hand position.)* He will always do this. *(Hands and arms outstretched.)*

This week, remember that Jesus cares about you and he wants to reach out to you. Find ways to use your hands to reach out to others. God bless you.

24. Traffic Signals

Scripture: Colossians 4:2

Concept: A traffic signal tells us to go, to slow down, or to stop. God answers our prayers in the same way.

Preparation: A picture or model of a traffic signal, if available.

Look what I've got today. *(Display picture.)* Do you know what this is? *(Children respond.)* This is a picture of a traffic signal. Do you know what the different colors mean? How about the light at the top, the red one, what does it mean? *(Children respond.)* It means "stop." It doesn't mean slow down a lot or go slow. It means "stop" all the way, so you are not moving. I know someone who *almost* stopped at a red light, but the tires on the car were still rolling just a little. There was a policeman nearby and my friend got a ticket for not stopping at a red light. Red means "stop."

How about the light in the middle, the yellow one? What does it mean? *(Children respond. You may have to offer help for this one.)* This means "yield." Yield is a word you may not hear very often. It means "slow down" and "look out for the other guy." When you yield, you may have to slow down and wait for someone else to go first.

You are doing a great job with this. I can tell you are going to be good drivers. The last light is easy. What does the green one mean? *(Children respond.)* "Go!" We all like that one, because we don't have to wait any longer.

Did you know that when we pray to God, he gives us answers like a traffic light? It's true. Sometimes we pray, and God says, "Stop." *(Point to the red light.)* God is telling us, "No." We may be asking God for something that is not good for us or for something that is not in God's plan for us. We may not like getting a red light from God, but when that happens, it's for our own good.

Other times when we pray, God says, "Yield, slow down." God is not saying, "No," but he is not saying, "Yes," either. When God gives us the yellow light *(point to the yellow light)* he wants us to take it easy and slow down a bit. Maybe it's not the right time for what we want. We may not like the yellow light any better than we like the red one, but if we trust God, we believe God knows what is best.

Most of us like the green light best. *(Point to the green light.)* When we get a green light from God, we know that God has said "Yes" to our prayer. We all like to get a "Yes."

A traffic signal is important when we are driving so we will know what to do and so we will be safe. God gives us answers to our prayers that help us know what to do and that lead us in the right way. God always knows what is best for us.

When you pray this week, pay attention to whether God says, "Stop," "Slow down," or "Go." God bless you.

25. Figuring The Answers

Scripture: Proverbs 3:5-6

Concept: A calculator can help us figure out math problems, but some things cannot be figured out. We believe them even though we don't understand them or have the answers.

Preparation: A hand-held calculator.

Have you ever used a calculator? You punch in a problem and the calculator figures the answer for you. Kind of neat, huh? Let's give it a try. 23 + 12. *(Put in the problem.)* Boom, the calculator says that 23 + 12 = 35. How about 103 - 22? *(Put in the problem.)* The calculator says 103 - 22 = 81. Someone give me a problem. *(Choose a volunteer. Make sure the problem is reasonable. Put in the problem.)* Here's your answer. Calculators make it simple to get the right answer every time. We don't have to do any work and we don't have to wait to have our question answered.

It's great to get fast and easy answers to our questions and problems, but some questions and problems don't have such easy answers. Sometimes we have to wait for answers, and some questions do not have an answer that we can understand.

Some people refuse to believe in God because they don't understand him. That is sad, isn't it? They don't have all the answers about the way God works so they say God must not be real. They ask, "If God is real, why do bad things happen?" "If God loves me, why do I have to hurt and suffer?" "How can God be real if there are so many mean people in the world who do so many bad things?" I don't have all the answers to their questions, but I still believe in God. I believe that God is good even when I don't understand everything that happens.

It's all right to ask questions. God does not mind, but some of our questions about him will never be answered. We have to choose to believe in him, to love him, and to follow him even if we don't understand everything he does. We have to trust God even when we don't have all the answers about him.

Unfortunately, there is no calculator that can give us the answers to our "God" questions. We really don't need that kind of calculator because we can choose to trust God even when we don't have all the answers.

When there is something about the Lord that you do not understand, remember that God has the answer, and that's all that matters. God bless you.

26. False Advertising

Scripture: Matthew 23:27-28

Concept: Just as television and commercials can mislead us, our behavior can mislead others concerning our relationship with the Lord.

Preparation: Watch Saturday morning television geared toward children and familiarize yourself with some of the commercials with outlandish claims designed to entice youngsters.

What is a commercial? *(Children respond.)* It's an advertisement about something that someone or some company is trying to sell. We see commercials on television and we find them in magazines and on the radio. The big billboards you see on the side of the road are commercials.

What is the purpose of a commercial? *(Children respond.)* Sometimes it seems the purpose of a commercial is to disturb our television show, doesn't it?! But commercials do have a purpose. They are trying to get our attention and make us buy whatever it is they are advertising.

Let's talk a little about some of the commercials you have seen. How about toy commercials? Who can tell me about a commercial for a toy that you have seen on television? *(Select several volunteers to share. Keep them on track.)* Commercials try to make us believe something.

Have you ever seen a commercial on television for something you really wanted? Maybe it was for a doll. In the commercial, the doll's hair was beautiful and silky. It looked so real! The commercial made it look like the doll could walk and talk just like a real baby. But when you got that doll home, the hair was frizzy and crinkled from being in the box and the doll would only walk if you moved her legs. That commercial let you believe something that was not true. What a disappointment!

Maybe you saw a commercial for a plane that would really fly! The boy in the commercial was having so much fun playing with his plane as it soared above the trees and around the yard; you couldn't wait to get your plane home so you could fly it! But when you got home from the store and tried to fly your plane, it would only go a little way before it fell to the ground. The commercial had only told part of the truth. Sometimes they are not completely honest with us. We have to be careful with commercials; sometimes, they stretch the truth.

Did you know that we are like commercials for God? It's true. When people know that we love, trust, and follow God, they watch us as if we were commercials. They see us go to church and sing hymns and pray. They see us go to Sunday School to study the Bible. They hear us say we believe we are supposed to live and act the way Jesus taught us to, *but* — *but,* then they watch the way we behave when we are away from church. They watch to see how we treat others and how we talk. They watch to see if we are loving, kind, and fair. Just like television commercials tell us about things we want to buy, our behavior tells other people what we believe about God.

It is disappointing when a commercial has not told the truth about something it is trying to sell. It is even more disappointing when we are bad commercials for the Lord.

Think of ways this week that you can be a truthful commercial for the Lord by treating others fairly, sharing, and being kind. God bless you.

27. Believing What God Says

Scripture: Genesis 6:22

Concept: We cannot believe everything we read or hear, unless it comes from God.

Preparation: Be prepared to tell the story of Noah and God's command to build the ark. (Genesis 6:9 and following.)

Have you ever heard someone say, "You can't believe everything you read," or "You can't believe everything you hear"? Most of the time, that is good advice. You can't believe everything you read or hear because people do not always tell the truth. Sometimes they exaggerate and sometimes they tell stories.

Suppose I told you that I was almost late this morning because a big, green alien came in my room and ate my alarm clock. Would you believe that? Of course not. I was almost late because I kept turning off the alarm until I ran out of time. What if you read in a magazine that you could get rich if you sent someone all the money you had? Would you believe that? I hope not. You have to be careful about what you read and hear; not everything is the truth.

You can't believe everything you read or hear *unless* God says it. People might try to trick us or they may even tell us lies, but if God says it, we can believe it.

Do you know the story about Noah and the ark? Noah lived in a time when people had become very mean and evil. God was sorry he had made them so he decided to get rid of them — all of them except Noah and his family. Noah was a good man who loved and obeyed God. He and his family were to be saved along with two of each kind of animal God had created. Everything and everyone else would be destroyed by a big flood.

God told Noah that it was going to rain. Not just a little drizzle, mind you, but enough rain to cause a big flood, enough rain to destroy the earth. It sounded hard to believe. But that didn't matter; God said it would happen and Noah *did* believe it.

God instructed Noah to build an ark so he and his family would be safe. What's an ark? *(Children respond.)* It's a big ship. I suspect Noah looked silly out there building a big boat, claiming a flood was coming when it wasn't even raining. Some of the mean people probably came around to laugh and make fun of Noah and his family. They might have said something like, "Hey, Noah, going on a cruise?!" "Why are you wasting your time building an ark, Noah, why don't you just buy an umbrella?!" "Noah, that ark looks like a box of animal crackers!" But Noah didn't pay any attention to them. Maybe they didn't believe what God had told Noah, but Noah believed it. He went right on doing what God had asked him to do.

Guess what happened? *(Children respond.)* It began to rain, and it rained and it rained and it rained. Before long, the flood waters came and destroyed everything, everything that is, except Noah, his family, and the animals. It happened just like God said it would. Noah had listened to God and now he was safe.

We cannot believe everything we read or hear unless we hear it from God. Read your Bible, say your prayers, and pay attention to what God is trying to tell you.

God bless you.

28. A Light In The Darkness

Scripture: Matthew 5:14-16

Concept: Even one light can make a big difference in the darkness.

Preparation: A flashlight.

Have you ever been someplace that is dark? I mean really dark. So dark you can't see your hand in front of your face? So dark someone could be standing five inches in front of you and you would never know? So dark you feel totally and completely alone?

When I was in college, I worked as a summer missionary at a camp in the mountains. We did all sorts of neat things. We went canoeing, hiking, and camping, but the neatest thing we did was caving. We wore hard hats to protect our heads and we wore long pants and long-sleeve shirts because it's cold inside a cave even when it's summertime on the outside. Most important of all, we each carried a flashlight. *(Turn on flashlight and shine the light on the floor.)*

As we made our way inside a cave, we would turn on our flashlights so we could see our surroundings. The caves we visited were cold, slimy, and muddy. Sometimes we had to slide in on our bellies, but once we got inside, all the cold and mud was worth it. We saw many types of formations that had been developing over thousands and thousands of years. Some of them looked like fried eggs; others looked like bacon and still others reminded us of strange and mysterious statues.

Each time we took a group of children into the cave, we would perform an experiment together. We would all turn off our flashlights and sit in the dark. This experiment helped us realize what life would be like if we had to live in total darkness. It was an eerie feeling. We could not see anything. There were no glimmers of light coming from outside. There was nothing to brighten the dark cave. It was scary.

After a few minutes, the leader would have one person turn on a flashlight. *(Shine the light across the children.)* What a feeling of relief! One little light was stronger than all that darkness! One flashlight made a huge difference in that dark place! With one light, we could see each other's faces *(quickly pass the light across their faces)* and we could tell which direction we were supposed to go. One light was enough to chase the darkness and scary feelings away.

Jesus said he was the Light of the world. He was the one who could come into our lives and brighten things up. He was the one who could make the dark places light again, and he could chase away the dark and scary feelings.

But Jesus also said that we were the lights of the world. We can make a difference in other people's lives. When they are sad or hurting, we can brighten things for them by sharing Jesus' love. When they are lonely and afraid, we can be a light by spending time with them and being their friend.

One little flashlight makes all the difference in a dark cave. One person who is willing to share Jesus' love can make all the difference in someone's life.

God bless you this week. Try to find a way to be a light to someone.

29. What Hat Do You Wear?

Scripture: Proverbs 20:11

Concept: The hat someone wears often tells us a great deal about the person. As Christians, we don't wear hats, but our behavior tells a lot about us.

Preparation: Several hats (authentic or toy) if possible: fireman, policeman, football helmet, etc. Use pictures, if necessary.

Look what I have this morning: all kinds of hats. What kind of job uses this hat? *(Put on a hat and allow children to respond. Repeat for as many hats as you have.)* The type of hat someone wears can tell us a lot about that person, can't it? What does this hat tell us? *(Put on a hat. Children respond.)* This fireman's hat tells us that the person who wears it fights fires. This person risks his life to save others.

How about this hat? *(Put on policeman's hat. Children respond.)* Policemen wear this kind of hat. Policemen are men and women who help keep us safe. They protect us and make sure that everyone obeys the law.

One more. What about this hat? *(Put on football helmet. Children respond.)* This hat is worn by a football player. A football player enjoys sports and likes the rough and tumble; a football player gives us entertainment.

Hats can tell us something about the people who wear them. A fireman's hat tells us the person who wears this hat *(hold up fireman's hat)* belongs to the fire department and this one *(policeman's hat)* tells us the owner belongs to the police department, and this one *(football helmet)* tells that the owner belongs to a football team.

But what about us, God's people? Is there any special hat that God's people wear to tell others about us? No, we don't have a special hat, or a uniform. So how do people know we belong to

God? *(Children respond.)* People know we belong to the Lord by how we act. They know we belong to God because we show God's love and forgiveness and because we try to help others in any way we can. People know we belong to God because we share him with them!

We don't have a special hat, so if others are to know we belong to the Lord, we have to show them!

Pray for one another this week. God bless you.

30. How Much Protection Do You Have?

Scripture: Psalm 119:9-11

Concept: The more we "cover" ourselves with God's word, the more protection we have against temptation to do wrong.

Preparation: At least one bottle of sunscreen or suntan lotion with the SPF plainly visible. Several bottles with differing SPF's would be helpful.

Do you know what this stuff is? *(Children respond.)* It's sunscreen. We used to call this suntan lotion, but now we don't care so much about getting a tan as we do about protecting ourselves from the sun. What does sunscreen do? *(Children respond. Offer help if necessary.)* It keeps us from getting burned by the sun. We spread it all over our bodies before we go outside and it helps us not get burned so quickly. If you've ever had a sunburn, you know how painful that can be. Sunscreen protects us from that kind of pain.

Let me show you something. *(Display SPF number.)* See this number? This number tells us how much protection we have. If the number is low, like two or four, we don't have much protection and we shouldn't stay out in the sun too long, but if the number is high, like thirty or forty-five, we're well-protected and we can stay out longer.

Wouldn't it be great if we had some kind of *sin* screen? Something we could rub on to protect us from sin? Something that would keep us from doing wrong things? That would be terrific, but we don't have anything like that. What we do have is the Bible. If I rub my Bible all over myself, will that keep me from doing wrong? Of course not!

How can the Bible protect me from sin? You see, the more we read the Bible and the more we learn about the way God wants us to live, the more we will choose to follow him instead of choosing to do wrong. If we only learn a little about the Bible, it's like using sunscreen with a low number. *(Display low number SPF lotion.)* We only get a little help, but if we study the Bible and learn as much as we can, it's like using the sunscreen with a high number *(display bottle)* and we get lots of help in choosing to do right instead of wrong.

I hope you use sunscreen when you're out in the sun so you won't get burned, but I especially hope you are using the Bible to give you help when you're tempted to do wrong, and to learn how to be the person God wants you to be.

I'll be praying for you this week. God bless you.

31. Do It To Them, Do It To Me

Scripture: Matthew 25:40, 45

Concept: Jesus teaches that the way we treat others is the way we treat him.

Preparation: Be familiar with Matthew 25:31-46.

(Before the service, enlist an adult seated near the front to help you.) This is Mr. _____ (or Mrs. _____). He/She will be helping us with our lesson this morning. If I walk up to Mr. _____ and punch him in the arm, who did I hit? *(Children respond. They may be a bit perplexed; offer help if needed.)* Who did I hit? That's a silly question, I hit Mr. _____, but who else did I hit? *(Children respond.)* No one? Are you sure?

Suppose I knock him down and steal his money, who did I knock down and steal from? *(Children respond.)* Mr. _____, are you sure? What if Mr. _____ was sick or hungry and I passed by him without helping? Who did I pass by? *(Children respond.)* Mr. _____? Again, are you sure?

Did you know the Bible teaches us when we do mean things to others, it's like we are doing mean things to Jesus? When I punch Mr. _____, it is like I hit Jesus. When I knock him down and steal his money, it's like I knock down Jesus and steal from him, and when I pass by Mr. _____ when he is sick or hungry, it's as if I were passing by Jesus if he were sick or hungry.

Did you ever think about your behavior that way? Did you realize that Jesus says the way we treat others is the way we treat him? When we ignore people who need our help, it's as if we are ignoring the Lord. When we don't share with others or when we are cruel and mean to them, it's as if we are doing these things to Jesus.

Would you ever hit Jesus? Would you be cruel to him or not share what you had with him? None of us would act like that, would we? But remember, Jesus said if we treat others that way, it's the same as treating him that way.

This is a tough lesson, isn't it? But it is an important one. This week, remember to treat others the way you would treat Jesus. God bless you.

32. All Tangled Up

Scripture: James 4:7

Concept: Sin sneaks up on us slowly, then all at once, it ensnares us.

Preparation: A spool of thread.

I need a helper this morning. *(Choose one youngster to assist. Position him/her where he/she can be seen by the congregation. Have the child extend his/her hands, wrists together, as you tie one loop of thread around the wrists while beginning to speak.)* Let's see how strong you are. Can you pull your wrists apart and break that thread? Sure you can, it's just a little piece of wimpy string. Anyone can break through that. Let's try this again. What if I wrap it around twice this time? *(Wrap and tie.)* Can you break that? A little harder, but you are still stronger than that thread. That thread can't hold you. It can't tie you up. One more time. What if I wrap it around five, six, or seven times this time? *(Wrap and tie.)* I'm not sure you can break this one.

You're finally tied up by the thread. It has caught you. You kept getting more and more tangled up by the string because it didn't catch you at first. You thought you could beat it, but finally it caught you.

This is how sin works in our lives. We start messing around with things we know are wrong because we think we are strong enough not to get tangled up with them. At first, we may not get caught. We might get away with a lot, but then, BAM! We're all caught up and we can't get out by ourselves. Like the loops of thread that we can't break through, sin will eventually catch us and tangle us up.

I've known boys and girls who started telling lies to get out of trouble. They told one or two lies and never got caught, so they lied again, and again, and again. But before long, their lies caught up with them. Not only did they get in trouble, but they had a hard time knowing what was the truth and what was a lie.

We all think that we are strong enough or smart enough not to get caught by sin. But if we keep playing around with things that are wrong, eventually they will catch us. Sin has a way of sneaking up on us and tangling us up when we don't expect it.

Be careful and don't play games with sin. Eventually, we will get caught. God bless you.

33. Doing What You Were Meant To Do

Scripture: Jeremiah 29:11

Concept: Don't let anything keep you from doing what you were meant to do.

Preparation: Felt-tip marker, white paper, and clear tape. Put a piece of clear tape over the writing tip of a felt-tip marker.

I'm not much of an artist, but I'm going to draw you a picture this morning. *(Begin drawing on the paper — of course, nothing happens because the ink can't flow.)* Something is wrong. I've got paper and I've got a marker, but the marker is not working correctly. Let's try again. *(Try to draw on the paper.)* It's still not working. Something is keeping this marker from doing what it's supposed to do.

Look at the tip of this marker. What do you see? *(Children respond.)* The tape is ruining this perfectly good marker. The tape is blocking the ink and keeping the marker from doing its job. What good is a marker that can't write or draw?

God has something special for each of us to do. It's important that we don't let anything keep us from doing what we are meant to do. God might want some of you to be teachers. If that is what God has for you, then don't let anyone or anything keep you from being the best teacher you can be. God might want others of you to be factory workers, missionaries, librarians, homemakers, preachers, doctors, salesmen, or who knows what, but whatever God has in store for you, you do it, and don't let anything stop you.

Remember this marker? *(Hold up marker for children to see.)* We don't want to be like this. As long as this marker lets the tape keep it from doing what it's supposed to do, it's no good. But if we get rid of the tape, the marker can do its job and do it well. I want to be like the marker without the tape, so I can do what I was meant to do.

Let God help you discover what it is you are meant to do and then don't let anything keep you from doing it.

God bless you. Have a good week.

34. A Fresh Start

Scripture: Romans 3:23-24

Concept: When we make mistakes, God will give us a fresh start if we ask him.

Preparation: A clean sheet of white paper, and a sheet of white paper with crayon scribbles on it.

If you were trying to draw a picture and messed up, you would want to start over, wouldn't you? *(Hold up paper with scribbles.)* Looks like someone made some mistakes here. Looks like he messed up a little bit. Do you think whoever started drawing this picture would like to start over? Do you think he would like to try again?

If this was your paper *(hold up paper with scribbles)*, would you want to draw your new picture on it? No, no one wants to draw a new picture on messy paper. We would want a fresh, clean sheet of paper, wouldn't we? *(Hold up clean sheet.)* We would want the chance to start over with a brand-new piece of paper that didn't have any marks on it so our new picture would be neat and pretty.

Believe it or not, our lives are like these sheets of paper. We start out like a nice, clean sheet of paper. But then, we make mistakes, we sin, we do things that hurt other people and hurt God, and our lives begin to look like the paper with all the messy scribbles on it.

The good news is that God can give us a fresh start. God can forgive the mistakes we make if we tell him we're sorry and ask him to forgive us. God can make our lives look like this clean sheet of white paper with no mistakes on it, so that we can start over.

Sometimes my life looks like this. *(Hold up paper with scribbles.)* I'm glad that God forgives me when I make mistakes and when I sin. I'm glad God gives me the chance to start over so my life looks like this! *(Hold up clean sheet.)*

This week, when you do something wrong or when you hurt someone, remember that you can start over. Remember that God will forgive you if you ask.

God bless you. I'll be praying for you.

35. Being Ready

Scripture: Matthew 24:36-44

Concept: It is important to be prepared because we never know what's coming.

Preparation: Be familiar with Matthew 24:36-44.

A few years ago, my sister and I went to the beach for the weekend. We stayed way up high on an upper floor of a hotel. We had a great time, swimming, shopping, watching dolphins jump, and just relaxing. But the last night we were there something frightening happened.

Very early in the morning, when it was still a little dark outside, an alarm went off in our hotel room. A loud speaker blared, "Attention! Attention! This is an emergency! Smoke has been detected on your floor. Find the nearest exit and leave immediately!" We were scared! We jumped out of bed so we could get dressed and get out of there.

But I was not ready for an emergency. I had not been careful with my clothes the night before and they were thrown all over the room. I could not find my shorts or my shirt. I couldn't find my shoes, my keys, or my pocketbook and there was no time to spare. Finally, I found something to put on and hurried down to safety. Because I wasn't ready, something bad could have happened.

It's important to be prepared. What happens at school when you are not ready for a test? *(Children respond.)* How about when you're playing baseball and someone pitches the ball before you're ready? *(Children respond.)* Suppose you were to go to a party and your mom gave you chores to do before you could go. You didn't do them and you were not ready when it was time to leave. What would happen? *(Children respond.)*

What happens if we're not ready to meet Jesus and learn about him? We'll miss out on something quite special. If we're not ready for Jesus, we may not learn how much he cares for us and loves us. If we're not ready for him, we might miss out on everything Jesus has for us.

We never know what's going to happen to us, but we need to be ready to face whatever comes our way. We can't wait too long to get ready or it may be too late.

Don't wait too long to get ready! Let's pray for one another this week. God bless you.

36. Big Sin, Little Sin

Scripture: Luke 6:37-42

Concept: Even though we judge sin as being big or little, in God's eyes, sin is sin.

Preparation: Tape measure, yardstick, or ruler.

I need a helper this morning. *(Choose a youngster to assist you.)* Let's see how tall you are. *(Measure height.)* You are getting tall. Stretch out your arm and let's measure that. *(Measure arm.)* No doubt about it, you are really growing.

We can measure all sorts of things: tables, rooms, walls, you name it and we can measure it. But what about sin? First of all, what is sin? *(Help children with appropriate responses.)* Sin is what we do wrong. Sin is what we do that hurts God or hurts other people. Sin could be telling a lie or stealing something; sin is being mean and cruel to others. We sin when we do those things we know are wrong.

So how do we measure sin? What sins are big and what sins are little? Is telling a lie a little sin and cheating on a test a big sin? Is it worse to hurt someone's feelings or to ignore someone who needs our help? Can we measure these things with our yardstick?

We try to measure sin. Sometimes we say, "At least what I did was not as bad as what she did!" We try to make our sin look little and someone else's sin look big. But the Bible teaches us that sin is sin, wrong is wrong. Even though some things might seem worse than others to us, in God's eyes, it's all the same. We really can't measure it. We can't say one sin is worse than another.

You see, God doesn't want us to waste time trying to figure out what sins are big and what sins are little. God doesn't want us to think our sins are somehow less important than someone else's sin. God wants us to spend our time choosing to do those things that will make him happy. God wants us to love him and to love others. If we really try to do that, we won't have time to worry about measuring sin.

God bless you. This week, see if you can find special ways to show God that you love him.

37. Stain Remover

Scripture: 1 John 1:9

Concept: We put stain remover on clothes to get rid of the dirt and grime, but the only stain remover that will get rid of our sin is Jesus Christ.

Preparation: A bottle or stick of laundry stain remover.

Do you know what this is? *(Children respond. Offer help if needed.)* It's stain remover. What does Mom or Dad do with this? *(Children respond.)* They rub it on the stains we get on our clothes. Have you ever gotten a stain on your shirt or your pants? What makes the worst stain? *(Children respond.)* How about grass stains on your knees? They are hard to get out, aren't they? What about grape juice on a white shirt, or chocolate syrup on a Sunday dress? What a mess!

Those stains need some extra help before they will come out of clothes. Mom or Dad takes the stain remover and rubs it all over the stain before they wash the clothes. *(Demonstrate.)* It dissolves the grime so it will wash away.

Why do we want to get rid of the stains? *(Children respond.)* Stains ruin the way our clothes look. We like to look neat and clean. We don't want to look dirty. Who wants old, nasty stains all over their clothes?

Did you know that we can get stains on the inside? We get inside stains when we sin. Does anyone know what sin is? *(Select a volunteer or offer the answer.)* Sin is what we do that hurts God. Sin is what we do wrong such as not telling the truth, fighting, stealing, and disobeying our parents. Whenever we sin, it is like leaving a big ugly stain on the inside.

(Display stain remover.) This works pretty well at getting the stains out of our clothes. But do you think it can get rid of the stain left by sin? No. Stain remover cannot do that.

There is only one way to get rid of stains on the inside. There is only one way to get rid of sin and that is by telling Jesus that we are sorry for what we have done wrong. If we really mean it when we say we are sorry, Jesus will forgive us. The stain on the inside will be removed and we will be clean again. Jesus is the best kind of stain remover!

When you say your prayers this week, tell Jesus you are sorry for the things you have done wrong and ask him to get rid of the stain on the inside. God bless you.

38. Trouble

Scripture: Psalm 34:14

Concept: Trouble is no game.

Preparation: A game board from the game "Trouble."

Can you read this word? *(Children read from the game.)* Trouble. Have any of you ever played the game "Trouble" before? You pop the dice to find out how many spaces to move around the board. *(Demonstrate.)* The object of the game is to go all the way around the board and get your game pieces into the home slot before others get to their home slot. It's fun. But if someone else pops a number and ends up in the same space as you, you're in TROUBLE and you have to start all over again. *(Demonstrate.)* Oh well, it's just a game.

We can find ourselves in trouble that is not a game and there is nothing fun about it. Have you ever been in trouble? *(Children respond.)* What kinds of things get us in trouble? *(Children respond.)* Not telling the truth, not cleaning your room when Mom asks, hitting your brother or sister, not doing your homework, running when you were supposed to be walking; gee, all kinds of things can get us into trouble.

What happens when we get in trouble? *(Children respond.)* Sounds like all kinds of things can happen when we are in trouble. At first, we are probably a little scared and nervous. We don't know what is coming, but we are afraid we're really going to get it. Then, we're sorry that we did wrong. We wish we could take it all back, but it's too late. We're in for it and there is no way out. Sometimes we have to sit in timeout, or we get grounded. Maybe we lose our allowance, cannot talk on the phone, or have our favorite toy taken away. There is usually some kind of consequence for getting in trouble.

Does it feel better to be in trouble or not in trouble? *(Children respond.)* Of course, it feels better not to be in trouble. How can we stay out of trouble? *(Children respond.)* We can stay out of trouble by doing what we are supposed to do and by not doing what we are not supposed to do. Sounds easy enough, but it can be hard sometimes. If we ask God to help us, he will. God will help us make choices and decisions that will keep us out of trouble.

Trouble is no game. *(Display the game board.)* There is always a price to pay. Life is a lot more fun and a lot easier if we make choices that please God and keep us out of trouble.

This week, pray that God will help you do the things that will keep you out of trouble. God bless you.

39. Too Close To The Edge

Scripture: Proverbs 4:14-15

Concept: It's a lot smarter to stay as far away from trouble as you can, rather than trying to see how close you can get to it without getting hurt.

Preparation: None.

I have a story for you today. There was once a king who was searching for the perfect husband for his daughter. The king was like any father. He wanted his daughter's husband to take care of her, love her, and protect her.

Finally, the king found three handsome, strong young men, each of whom was a possible husband for the lovely princess. The king had a test to see which of the young men was most suited for his daughter.

There was in the kingdom a very dangerous stretch of road with narrow passageways, loose rocks, and steep, deadly cliffs. Anyone who went over the cliffs would surely die. The king's test for each man involved a challenge. After giving each one a wagon and horses, the king said, "This is my challenge. I wish to see how close each of you can come to the edge without falling over the cliff."

The wise king stood back and the test was begun. The first young man came barreling around the bend, horses at full speed. He came about this far from the edge *(hold arms about two feet apart)* and continued down the road, proud of himself for how well he had done. The king watched in silence.

The second young man, full of hope that he would win the king's confidence, and the princess' hand in marriage, brought his team of horses around the turn even more quickly than the first. He came breathtakingly close to the edge *(hold hands about six inches apart)* and knew that he had come closer to the edge than the first man. Surely he would be the winner. Again, the king watched in silence.

The third young man, as he approached the bend, instead of speeding up, slowed his horses down and as he passed the cliff, moved as far away from the edge as possible. The king raised his eyebrows in surprise.

Guess which fellow won the king's test? *(Children respond.)* The one who got this close? *(Hold hand apart about two feet.)* No. The man who got this close? *(Hold hands about six inches apart.)* No. The one who got away from the danger was the one the king chose.

The king wanted a husband for his daughter who would take care of her and protect her, not one who would put her at risk by playing with danger. The other two men were too reckless. They took too many chances. The king didn't care how close to the edge they could get; he wanted to see how far they would go to protect his daughter.

Many times, we try to see how close to the edge we can get before we fall over. We play with trouble until we have gone too far. It's a lot smarter and a lot safer to stay as far away from trouble as we can.

This week, don't try to see how close you can get to trouble but see how far away you can stay from it. God bless you.

40. Change

Scripture: Isaiah 43:19

Concept: Change may be difficult, but it can be a good thing.

Preparation: None. *(Stand in a different place in the sanctuary or shift something that the children will be sure to notice.)*

Do you notice anything different this morning? Has anything been changed? *(Children respond that you are standing in a different place.)* Put on your thinking caps and think with me this morning. What kind of things do we change? *(Allow children to respond. Prompt them if necessary.)* We change our socks. We change our clothes. We change our sheets. We change a baby's diaper. We change our minds. It is not difficult to change any of these things.

But sometimes things change and we don't have any control over them. A friend moves away. Your favorite cartoon does not come on television anymore. You grow a year older and have to move to a new Sunday School class and leave behind the teacher you love. These kinds of changes can be hard to handle at first, but they are not necessarily bad.

If your friend moved away, you would be sad, but it might give you the chance to make new friends. If your favorite cartoon stopped coming on television, maybe you would choose to read a story or draw a picture. When you move to a new Sunday School class, you will miss your old teacher, but you will have the chance to meet, learn from, and love a new teacher.

Just think how things would be if nothing ever changed. You would always be the same age. You would wear the same clothes, eat the same food, watch the same television show over and over, play the same game. Life would get boring, wouldn't it? Change may be difficult, but it keeps life fresh and exciting.

God knows that it is hard for us to deal with change, but God is with us to help us see that change can be a good thing. God can help us find something good about change, even when it is difficult.

This week ask God to help you make the best of difficult changes in your life. God bless you.

41. Serendipity!

Scripture: Matthew 6:33

Concept: There are many great treasures to be uncovered along the way, if we only open our eyes and our hearts to recognize them.

Preparation: None.

There are some words in the English language that are just plain fun to say and hear. These words roll off our tongues and tickle our ears. Our lesson this morning concerns one of these words. The word is "serendipity."

Isn't that a neat word? Serendipity. Say it with me, "serendipity." A serendipity is something really special that you find when you didn't even know you were looking for it. Sound confusing? It's not. Suppose you went into the attic to find an old game that you had packed away. While you were hunting for the game, you uncovered a baseball card that belonged to your dad when he was a boy. And not just any card, but one that was worth a lot of money. That would be a serendipity: something really special that you found when you were actually looking for something else.

Or imagine you were going on a hiking trip with your scout troop to learn about different kinds of trees and plants. Along your hike, you saw a beautiful deer, playful squirrels, and even an eagle. They would be serendipities.

Let's say you were on your way to the beach. You were so excited and couldn't wait to get there but you just hated the long drive. Even though you were in a hurry to get to the beach, your family stopped along the way to eat dinner and spend the night. There in the hotel you met a wonderful man who told funny stories and made you laugh. He became your friend. You guessed it. He was a serendipity.

We can't go looking for a serendipity, because when we look for it, it's never there. It is something we stumble onto quite by accident when we're looking for something else. Some people never come across serendipities. Not because they aren't there, but because some people are too busy, or hard-headed, or stubborn to notice them. Suppose when you were looking for your game in the attic, you threw the baseball card away without looking at it, or when you went on the hike, you didn't even notice the deer, squirrels, and eagle. What if you had not taken time to make friends with the funny man in the hotel? Look what you would have missed by not taking time to appreciate the serendipities around you.

God has created a big world for us to enjoy. We hurry along our way missing so much around us. We miss the serendipities because we won't take the time to appreciate them.

Do what you have to do, but don't get so busy that you don't have time to enjoy the special things along the way. God bless you.

42. Expectations

Scripture: Romans 15:7

Concept: People should be able to expect the church to be a place that is warm, kind, accepting, and fair.

Preparation: None.

How many of you love to go to school? Raise your hands. Suppose you loved to go school. You loved to read and write, do math problems and science experiments. School was your all-time favorite place to be. Let's suppose summer was about to end and it was time to go back to school. You couldn't wait to do all those neat "school" things that you enjoyed doing. But when you got to school you found there would be no reading and writing, no math and no science. Instead you were simply going to sit at your desk all day and listen to music. That would be a letdown. That's not what school was meant to be and it would not be what you had expected.

Suppose you wanted to be on the football team. You liked wearing the uniform and tackling other people. You liked running and throwing and catching the ball. But when you got to football practice, the coach said there would be no uniforms or running or catching or tackling. You were not actually going to play football. Instead you were going to listen to other people tell you about playing football for the whole season! That would be disappointing, wouldn't it? It would not be what you had expected.

Imagine you went to the toy store and only found books. Don't we have the right to expect a toy store to have toys? If it says it's a toy store, shouldn't it be like a toy store?

How about a church? People who have never been to church do not always know what to expect. Most of them expect that if they come to a church, the church people will be nice, friendly, and accepting. They expect that they can come to worship God even if they do not look like everyone else or dress like everyone else. They *should* be able to expect these things.

You would be disappointed if you went to school and it was not what you expected school to be, or if you went to football practice and there was something else in its place, or if you went to the toy store and there were no toys. People coming to church hoping to find God's loving, kind, and fair people will be terribly disappointed if they get to church and find people who are unkind and cruel.

Let's make sure that people looking to find God and God's people always find exactly what they are looking for at our church. God bless you.

43. Gifts For Mom

Scripture: Proverbs 31:28

Concept: Mothers deserve our thanks and admiration for a job well-done.

Preparation: A sheet of paper and a pen or marker.

Today is a special day for us. Who knows what today is? *(Children respond.)* Yes, indeed, today is Mother's Day. Why do we celebrate Mother's Day? *(Children respond.)* We celebrate Mother's Day to tell our mothers we love them and that we are thankful for everything they do for us.

For our time together this morning, we are going to write a Mother's Day letter to Mom and talk about some gifts we can give her. I brought paper and pen and you are going to tell me what to write. How should we begin our letter? *(Children respond.)* Dear Mom.... *(Put the children's ideas into short notes that you can jot down quickly. Help them include elements of thanks and gratitude, love, and appreciation, and a few specifics. Don't worry about the organization of the letter. You will read it to the mothers in the congregation when it is finished.)*

You've said many nice things. This is a wonderful letter. I'm going to read it to all the moms in the congregation. *(Read the letter.)*

We've written a Mother's Day note, but what about a Mother's Day present? Anybody got some money so we can go buy some Mother's Day gifts? Oh no, what shall we do? If we don't have money to buy Mom a gift, what can we give her on her special day? *(Children respond.)* Someone said we could make a gift, and that's a great idea. What else could we do, any ideas? *(Children respond.)* We can give Mom some gifts that don't cost money. We could give Mom a present by not misbehaving during the rest of the worship service. We could give her a gift by not talking back or fighting with our little brother or sister today. She would count it a special gift if we did what we were told without whining or complaining. The most precious gift we could give her today is a big hug. Let's be sure to tell her how glad we are that she is our mom.

There are many gifts we can give Mom, but the best gifts come from our hearts, not from a store. Remember that today is her day, and we need to do everything we can to let her know she is loved, wanted, and appreciated.

Be sure to say a special prayer for your mother today. I'll pray for you this week and you pray for me. God bless you.

44. Thanks, Dad

Scripture: Exodus 20:12

Concept: Father's Day is a time to thank Dad.

Preparation: None.

There are many special days in a year and today is one of those days. Who knows what today is? *(Children respond.)* Today is Father's Day. We take time today to thank our fathers for all they do. I know some boys and girls don't have fathers; that might make you feel sad today, but if you don't have a father, you can thank someone who is like a father to you. This morning, I want to tell you a story about my father.

This is a true story that happened when I was a little girl. My family was camping in the mountains and we decided to go on a hike. This hike started out at the top of a mountain and wound around and around down the mountainside. It was a long way down, but going down wasn't so bad. As a little girl, however, I didn't remember that if I went all the way down, I would have to climb all the way back up.

Once we reached the bottom, we were near the foot of a tremendous waterfall. Boy, was it magnificent! The water crashed down and exploded all over us. We could feel the cool spray on our faces. It was quite a sight but I was tired after that long hike down and I really didn't care about waterfalls. After a while, my dad said it was time to head back to the top. Back to the top? Did Daddy expect me to hike back up that mountain? I couldn't do it! I knew I'd never make it! I was too tired to climb a mountain! I was just a little kid!

Sobbing and feeling sorry for myself, I took a few steps, but I *really* was too tired and too little to complete such a steep climb. I didn't have the strength. Finally, I plopped down in the middle of the path, put my head down on my chest, and cried. My dad could have gotten angry. He could have said if I was big enough to hike down then I was big enough to hike up. But instead, he came and picked me up. He carried me until I was rested and able to climb on my own.

My Dad didn't know it back then, and neither did I, but he taught me a lesson about God that day. He taught me that we get ourselves into places that we can't get out of, and that sometimes we are too weak to go on, but during those times, God picks us up, carries us, and lets us rest until we are strong enough to continue.

I learned a lot from my parents. Today, Father's Day, let's be sure to say, "Thanks, Dad." Remember to let your dad know how much you love him and appreciate him. God bless you.

45. Remembering Something Important

Scripture: 1 Corinthians 11:23-26

Concept: Communion is a time of remembering what Jesus has done for us.

Preparation: Several photographs.

Have you ever taken a picture of someone or something? Why do we take pictures, what good are they? *(Children respond.)* Photographs help us remember special times, places, and people. Here are some of my favorite photographs. *(Share pictures with the children and personalize the story to fit your photos.)* These are my five sisters. This picture helps me remember the first time we all went on vacation together. We went to the beach and had an awesome time with one another. This is my dog, Eli. This photograph reminds me of the first time Eli got a bath. What a mess! This last picture is of my grandparents. It helps me remember all the special times I had with them when I was growing up. Photographs are like treasures. We can look at a picture and remember all about something special that happened in our lives.

Communion at church is kind of like that. *(Display the elements, if appropriate.)* We eat the bread and drink the juice to help us remember the very special things that Jesus Christ did for us. Can you remember what Jesus did to forgive our sin? *(Children respond.)* Jesus died on the cross for our sin. I know that is difficult to understand. The grown-ups don't understand it all either, but we believe it.

The bread helps us remember Jesus' body which was hung on the cross and the juice reminds us of his blood. The service allows us to remember that Jesus did what he did because he loved us and he wanted us to have a better life now and a special life with God after we die.

Communion can be hard to understand, but remember that, just like a picture, communion is a special time that helps us remember everything Jesus did for us.

Be good to one another this week. God bless you.

46. Rise Again!

Scripture: Matthew 28:5-6

Concept: Jesus arose from the dead, just as he said!

Preparation: "Trick" (relighting) birthday candles, matches, and a damp paper towel. *You will need to practice this to get your timing down, but the results will be worth the effort!*

I want you to watch my hands as I talk this morning. Are you watching? Today is a very special day. It's Easter Sunday, probably the most special day of the year for Christian people. It is the day we remember that Jesus came to earth, lived with us, died for our sins, and, most importantly of all, arose from the dead.

Are you watching my hands? Do you remember how Jesus died? *(Children respond.)* He died on a cross, then he was buried. He was alive *(light the candle and display for all to see)*, and then he was crucified. They killed him. Jesus was dead. *(Blow out the candle but continue to hold it up.)*

(Most of these candles take between twenty and thirty seconds to relight. Practice with the same candle several times to know how much time you have to speak.)

But that is not the end of the story. Jesus had said that he would die, but he also said he would rise again. Many people did not believe him. Jesus *did* die, he was buried deep in the earth and his grave was sealed with a huge stone. But he was not going to stay dead. The grave and that big rock could not hold him because God had other things in mind.

Hey! Did you see that! It's amazing! *(The candle should have relit. Hold the candle high so all can see it.)* Just as I put out the candle and it relit so mysteriously, Jesus was put to death and raised to new life by God. The candle was out but now it's burning; Jesus was dead but now he's alive! We don't know *how* God did it, but we are glad *that* God did it.

And now, because Jesus is alive, we know that we can have a relationship with him. We know that he loves and cares for us and wants to help us live happy lives that please God. Jesus is alive and that's the reason we celebrate today!

I hope you have a blessed Easter Sunday. God bless you.

47. The Messenger

Scripture: Luke 2:8-14

Concept: Angels served as messengers for the good news that Jesus had been born. Now, we can be the messengers who share that message with all.

Preparation: An angel figurine or ornament. *(If you're more ambitious, you may want to dress as an angel.)*

    Christmas is coming! You can feel it in the air. The stores are decorated, radio stations play carols, and there are candles in the windows. But I wonder if people know about Christmas, I mean *really* know about Christmas? I wonder if they know the message of Christmas?
    Isn't this a lovely angel? I hang it on my tree each year. I have lots of angel decorations because angels played an important part in the Christmas story. Do you know what angels do? *(Children respond.)* Angels have several jobs, but most of the time angels serve as messengers. They bring a message from God.
    How about the angels in the Christmas story? Do you remember what they did? *(Children respond. Offer help if needed.)* An angel came to Mary, to Joseph, and to the shepherds. What did the angel say? The angel told Mary she would have a baby and that the baby would be God's son. The angel told Joseph not to be afraid and to believe the story Mary told him. The angels came to the shepherds out in the field and they had exciting news, good news for the whole world! Do you remember what the angel told the shepherds? *(Children respond.)* The angel told the shepherds not to be afraid because he was bringing news of great joy.
    The angel said that Jesus had been born in Bethlehem. This was good news because Jesus was the Savior of the world.

God still has angels, but now he can also use us as messengers to help share the news that Jesus is alive. We can tell others that they no longer need to be afraid, lonely, or sad because Jesus, the Savior, can help. He is the one who can change our lives, and that really is good news!

This Christmas season, be a messenger and share the Good News! God bless you.

48. I'm Somebody!

Scripture: Luke 2:8-11

Concept: Everybody is *somebody* with Jesus.

Preparation: A shepherd figurine or ornament.

    Look at my little shepherd friend here. *(Display figurine/ornament.)* What do you know about shepherds? *(Children respond.)* They took care of sheep. They lived out in the field with the flock. Let's think about this. If shepherds lived out in the field with a bunch of sheep, where did they sleep and where did they take a bath?
    Hmm ... they must have been dirty and smelly. In biblical times, people didn't pay much attention to shepherds. Shepherds did their job and left everyone else alone. No one thought a shepherd was worth worrying about. They didn't make much money, they weren't very clean, and they lived with animals. They just didn't matter a great deal to anyone. They were unimportant.
    But that all changed one night when the shepherds were out in the field watching their sheep. Suddenly, an angel appeared to the them and told them that Jesus Christ had been born in Bethlehem. This was the most important news in the world and the angel told the shepherds about it first!
    Imagine that. Here were shepherds who didn't matter to anybody. Shepherds who no one cared about or paid any attention to, and yet God decided they should be the first ones on earth to receive the good news that Jesus had been born.
    That tells us something about God. It tells us that God doesn't care how much money we have. God doesn't care where we live or what we look like. He doesn't care what kind of job we have as long as it's honest. God doesn't even care if no one else thinks we

matter, because we matter to him. We might be "nobodies" to everyone else, but each of us is a "somebody" to God.

God could have sent his angel to the kings and rich people first, but he chose to deliver his precious message to the lowly shepherds.

When you are feeling small and as if you do not matter, remember the shepherds and remember that you will always matter to God. Merry Christmas and God bless you.

49. Giving What You've Got

Scripture: Luke 2:1-7

Concept: The innkeeper is accused of turning away the Savior, but actually he gave what he had to give. We are called to do the same.

Preparation: None.

Help me remember some of the characters from the Christmas story. There's Mary, Joseph, shepherds, angels, anyone else? How about the innkeeper? What do you remember about him? *(Children respond.)* The innkeeper told Mary and Joseph there was no room for them in his inn. Sometimes when we hear about this fellow, we hear people say negative things about what he did. They say, "He had no room for Jesus," or "The innkeeper had no room for the Savior." Because he had no room in his inn for Mary, Joseph, and the baby, some people say that he must not have had any room in his heart for Jesus either. But that's not fair.

That innkeeper couldn't help it if so many other people got to Bethlehem before Mary and Joseph. It wasn't his fault the inn was full, and after all, he didn't really turn them away, did he? No, he let them stay in the stable with the animals. It wasn't much, but it was the only place available in Bethlehem that night. The innkeeper didn't have a lot to give, but he gave what he had.

There are times when all of us feel that we have nothing to give Jesus or his church. We don't have much money, we feel that our talents are not as important as someone else's, or we think that Jesus couldn't possibly need anything we have to give. But the truth is Jesus wants us to give what we have. If I can care for babies in the nursery, then that is what I should give to the Lord and his church. If I can pick up trash in the church parking lot, that is what I should give. If you can sing a song that will praise God, that is a gift you can share.

You see, the gift we can give Jesus or his church does not have to be expensive or impressive. It just has to be what we can give. My gift and your gift and the innkeeper's gift will not be the same, but it will please the Lord if we give it from our heart.

The innkeeper gave what he had. That's what Jesus wants from us. God bless you.

50. Don't Forget Jesus

Scripture: Luke 2:10-11

Concept: We miss Christmas altogether if we forget about Jesus.

Preparation: A creche with several figurines.

In my family, we love to decorate for Christmas. We like all the candles, angels, and ornaments, and we enjoy collecting Christmas decorations from year to year. I collect nativity scenes. *(Display the creche.)* I wanted to share this one with you today.

A nativity scene can help us remember what the Christmas story is all about. Let me demonstrate. Would you help me with these figures? *(Pass out all the figurines except baby Jesus.)*

Does anyone have the angel? The angel came and told Mary that she would be the mother of God's son. An angel also came to Joseph in a dream and told him not to be afraid and to make Mary his wife. Angels appeared one more time in the story, on the night Jesus was born. An angel came to the shepherds and told them that the savior of the world had been born in Bethlehem.

Who's got Mary? Mary was a young woman chosen by God to be the mother of God's son. She must have been afraid and confused when the angel came to her, but she was an obedient young lady and she trusted God.

Where's Joseph? Joseph was Mary's husband and he would be Jesus' father here on earth. What a responsibility Joseph had!

It seems to me there were lots of animals in this story. Does anyone have animals? There were animals in the stable where Jesus was born in Bethlehem. You remember, there was no room in the inn so Mary and Joseph had to stay in the stable with the animals.

There, isn't that a great story? I told you the nativity scene could help us remember. What's the matter? Something's missing? What's missing? *(Children respond.)* Jesus is missing! There is no Christmas without Jesus. *(Put the baby Jesus in the center of the creche.)* All the other characters don't really matter if we forget about the Lord.

Boys and girls, Christmas comes each year and we get all excited about the gifts, the parties, and the presents, but we miss Christmas altogether if we forget that Jesus is the reason we celebrate. He came to earth for us and if we leave him out of our Christmas celebrations, there is no Christmas.

I hope you have a blessed Christmas season, with Jesus at the center of everything you do. God bless you.

51. The Best Presents

Scripture: Matthew 1:21

Concept: Santa Claus is no match for Jesus! The gifts Jesus brings are eternal.

Preparation: A Christmas ornament or figurine of the baby Jesus (from a nativity scene) and of Santa Claus.

Look what I've got here. Who is this? *(Display figurines. Children respond.)* Of course, this is the baby Jesus. How about this one? Everyone knows who Santa is. Now, let me ask you a question. I want you to think about the answer before you speak, and I want you to be honest. Here's my question. Who gives the best Christmas presents, Santa Claus or Jesus?

Santa gifts are lots of fun! Trucks, cars, dolls, tea sets, video games, stereos, new clothes, all kinds of stuff to play with! Santa gifts are great, but what about the gifts that Jesus gives?

What kinds of gifts *does* Jesus give us? *(Children respond. Direct their answers, if necessary.)* Jesus gives us hope, peace, love, strength, rest, joy, and all the things that really matter in life. Jesus can give us what we need to live a happy life.

What happens to the Santa gifts after we play with them for a while? *(Children respond.)* The batteries wear out, or we get tired of them and toss them aside, or they break and don't work like they're supposed to anymore. But the gifts that Jesus gives never break down. They don't need batteries and they will last forever.

There really is no contest, Jesus gives the best presents. We all like the Santa gifts and they are fun to get and to give, but they don't compare to the wonderful, life-changing gifts that Jesus Christ gives. I hope you enjoy your Santa gifts, but I pray that you treasure your Jesus gifts!

I hope you have a blessed Christmas season. God bless you.

52. A Birthday Party

Scripture: Luke 2:11

Concept: Christmas is a celebration of Jesus' birth, yet we get all the presents.

Preparation: Birthday party supplies — hat, noisemaker, etc.

(Put on the hat and blow the noisemaker.) We're having a birthday party! What fun! Have you ever had a birthday party? *(Children respond.)* What kinds of things do you do at a birthday party? *(Children respond.)* You play games, eat cake and ice cream, run around with your friends, sing "Happy Birthday," and get presents.

How would you like to have your very own birthday party on your very own birthday, but everyone else got all the presents? What would you think of that? *(Children respond.)* Don't think you'd like that too much? Me neither. Doesn't sound like much fun, does it? Other people getting all the presents on your birthday. That's just not right. It's not fair.

Guess what? That happens to Jesus every year on his birthday. Really. His birthday comes around and we spend lots of time worrying about gifts, but many times we forget that Christmas is Jesus' birthday, not ours. Maybe we should spend more time giving Jesus gifts at Christmas.

Jesus probably doesn't care about video games or mittens or toys, but what kinds of things can we give him for his birthday? *(Children respond.)* We could give him our time by reading our Bibles and praying more often. We could give him our love by loving others. Maybe we could go to a nursing home and share love with some older folks who may be lonely. We could clean out our dresser drawers and closets and give the clothes to some people who really need them. We could help Mom and Dad around the house. There are lots of ways to give to the Lord. You see, the way we give to Jesus is by giving to others. If we want to celebrate his birthday, we have to do things for him, things that will make him happy.

This Christmas, remember that it's Jesus' birthday we're celebrating. He's the one who should get all the attention, not us. God bless you and Merry Christmas!